YOU'VE GOT ME SINGING THE BLUES

Steve Chambers

DRAMA EDITIONS

First published 1988 by IRON press
5 Marden Terrace, Cullercoats,
North Shields, Tyne & Wear (091) 253 1901.

Printed by Tyneside Free Press Workshop
5 Charlotte Square, Newcastle upon Tyne

© Copyright 1988 Steve Chambers

Typeset in 10pt. Times by Roger Booth Ass.
18–20 Dean St., Newcastle upon Tyne NE1 1PG

Front cover design by Clare Brannen

Book paste-up by Rachel Levitas

ISBN 0–906228 32 8

This play is copyright and therefore should not be performed legally or read before an audience without a license. Please apply to the publishers.

IRON Press books are represented by Password (Books) Ltd., 25 Horsell Rd. London N5 1XL. Tel: (01) 607 1154

supported by NORTHERN ARTS

Steve Chambers grew up in Nottingham and went to University in London. He has lived in Newcastle upon Tyne for the last sixteen years.

He is an active member of the Northern Playwrights' Society and has worked extensively in the North-East with both amateur and professional groups: Northumberland Theatre Company, Tynewear TIE, Bruvvers and Live Theatre Co., as well as Wallsend Young Peoples' Theatre, Peterlee Youth Drama Workshop and Newcastle Youth Theatre. A good deal of his work has been for young people and for three and a half years, Steve was director of Wallsend Youth Theatre before running the Live Youth Theatre for a further eighteen months. He was recently commissioned by Avon Touring Theatre Co. in Bristol and is currently co-writing a comedy drama for Central TV with Shaun Prendergast.

This is the second of Steve's plays to be published by *IRON PRESS*. *THE LAIDLEY WORM OF BAMBURGH* was commissioned by Northumberland Theatre Company as their Christmas Show in 1981 and published in 1982. *You've Got Me Singing the Blues* was written during Steve's tenure as recipient of the C.P. Taylor Bursary, an award set up by Northern Playwrights in memory of the North-East's best known playwright.

AUTHOR'S NOTES

BACKGROUND
While visiting a mental health hostel in Northumberland, I was told of how the day before they had seen a man in the grounds running across the grass towards the building only to stop suddenly, bend down examine the grass and then look up with a worried expression on his face. He ran to the wall of the building, bent down, appeared to listen and then paced carefully out onto the grass. Thinking they had a disturbed individual on their hands, a member of staff went outside to talk to the man. He was not a patient, he was the architect who was highly concerned that the drains had been sunk in the wrong place.

Difficult attitudes have traditionally been dismissed by authority as symptoms of madness and madness is associated with notions of magic, darkness and evil. Disturbed individuals present their opinions, obsessions and perceptions in a way which provides a deep insight into human existence. Desperation, being 'close to the edge' gives rise to a powerful oratory even when inarticulate. For a long time, I had wanted to write a play which contained so called 'mad' people at the start but as it progressed, the audience would begin to relate to the characters as individuals they cared about. Hopefully, by the end of the play, the audience would be left with the contradiction of their own prejudices and what they had just experienced. That was what I wanted to do.

RESEARCH
First Impressions

'All mental illness is a rational response to the intolerable.'
This was my somewhat arrogant, philosophical starting-point but then practicality intervened. I was asked if I would be interested in running a writing workshop at a club for schizophrenics. I said I would and thus my research began. The theoretical certainty with which I approached the idea evaporated when confronted by real people. I didn't know what schizophrenia was, I didn't know how to approach them or how to run a writing course that would be helpful to them. The public view of them was soon impressed upon me. 'I suppose you'll be in two minds about going...' or 'I've half a mind to come with you' my friends would say laughing when I told them I was off to work at the club. However, the schizophrenics themselves cracked gags about their illness frequently. One man came to me and said 'I used to be schizophrenic but we're alright now... hah hah hah'. Like everyone else in the club, I laughed with him.

Creative Writing

I dislike the term creative writing, it seems immediately to imply the opposite. Of course there is craft and technique associated with writing but for most people, the major problem is to unlock the door into themselves; everyone has a story to tell. For the first meeting we held a discussion. The first thing that struck me was how competitive everyone was. No-one wanted to listen to anyone else and everyone seemed keen to impress me. Even at that first meeting, the complaints began. 'Why aren't we writing? When are we going to do some writing?' They had had another tutor before me, a woman called Bushy who was soon invoked in every critical judgment of my work – 'Bushy wouldn't have wasted time like this...' 'Bushy was much easier to talk to...', 'Bushy liked my work more than you do'. My interest in writing was to encourage them to express themselves and most of them wanted to write but they wanted a competitive atmosphere where one of them was told that they were the best writer in the class. I said I was not interested in doing that; they did not approve and neither I was assured would Bushy have done. I could see that they didn't really think I was a proper writer, not like Catherine Cookson; they became restless. They asked me again what I had written and shook their heads as they agreed that none of them had ever heard of me. They weren't surprised, they were diagnosed schizophrenics, a famous writer wouldn't work with them; they got what they were used to, the second-rate and the second-hand.

I soldiered on, pushing the idea that they should express themselves, tell their stories. A crucial and in the end crippling insight occurred during a session in which I was 'brainstorming' the construction of a story. I explained that stories are journeys of discovery made up of dramatic episodes in which conflicts are resolved usually between heroes and villains, right and wrong, good and evil. I was giving examples when one of the group interrupted me. He could never do that. 'Do what?' I asked. He could never write stories that contained good and evil. I asked him why. He said that when he'd been working before his breakdown, there had been a black cloud of evil hovering behind him; he didn't want to write about evil. He sat with his arms folded in a posture of absolute certainty. I tried to continue but I realised that the kind of writing workshop I wanted to do could never work. I said before that my approach to creative writing was to get people to unlock the door into themselves and tell their stories. But that was the very last thing these people wanted to do; far from unlocking the door, they wanted it bolted tight shut forever. The door into themselves had come open of its own accord and they had seen their own darkness inside, they never wanted to see it again. I stopped trying to get my diminishing group to write after that. I took in stories and poems to read and discuss but even that came to seem a bogus activity. What was I – a cultural missionary saving them from their ignorance? I had already discovered that they knew much better than I did what my writing workshops could achieve, they had always known.

I stopped being a tutor and began attending the club like any other member, chatting to friends, playing pool, drinking coffee, arguing about politics and religion. Their conversation was perfectly ordinary except that it was littered with references to their latest medication and the precise behavioural vocabulary of the mental health professional. It was slightly unnerving to be asked 'What do you think of my social skills?' as I was after a game of pool. As I got to know them, I began to see them not as sick but as dispossessed. The fortunate ones had families that cared and still supported them to a lesser or greater extent. The unfortunate ones had no-one. Their illness had fractured all their relationships. Living in the community alone meant (and still means) being poverty stricken. With no money, there is little to do and few places to go apart from the round of 'drop-in' centres run by various charities for the homeless, the jobless, addicts and the chronically sick. Dealing with the mandarin complexities of the Supplementary Benefits regulations is difficult enough if one is well and clear thinking; in many cases for them it was a lottery. Some received invalidity benefit because they were deemed incurable, a diagnosis of damning hopelessness. Others were forced to apply for support as able bodied but temporarily sick individuals. Some had psychiatric social workers, others didn't. All were made to feel ultimately that they were in some sense to blame for their illness, that they were bad people and that their existence was a punishment for what they had done. I became more and more interested in the illness itself; what was it, how did it work?

What is Schizophrenia?

The schizophrenics themselves told me that they had something wrong with their brain; typically pointing to their head as they said this. When I asked them to explain further, they would say things like their brain went haywire, out of control but mostly they didn't want to talk about it. One expert told me that it's like your mind is out of your control. Thoughts occur to you unbidden and take unexpected pathways and one of the first external symptoms of a schizophrenic attack is, understandably, extreme anxiety, fear and terror. Other experts told me that schizophrenia was caused by a chemical imbalance in the brain, perhaps genetic; at any rate, heredity was a strong factor. Why couldn't the severe emotional disturbance be the cause of the chemical imbalance I asked. After all, there are physical changes when people get upset, angry, depressed. Why shouldn't severe disturbance cause severe chemical change? These suggestions were always dismissed without explanation. So many people told me with such certainty that schizophrenia was a physiological condition that I began to think that they must be correct. However, a physiological test for diagnosis has not been developed and the imprecise instrument of behaviour interpretation remains the major diagnostic tool. Surveys have shown that certain groups in society have a much higher incidence of diagnosis than others. Poor people are between three and eight times more likely to be diagnosed as are a much larger proportion of afro-caribbean people allowing some undiagnosed individuals to cite this as evidence of racial inferiority. The hearing of spirit voices is a common experience in afro-caribbean culture as is the inspection of newly completed buildings for architects. Unfortunately, hearing voices is a major diagnostic indicator for schizophrenia in the UK. There are more women in mental hospitals than men – why? Some experts argue it is because they live longer but the admission rate still shows significantly more women than men. A male Senior Clinical Nursing Officer informed me that it was because women were either more sensible than men and asked for help earlier or that they were weaker. This penetrating analysis smacks of the philosophy of the tabloid newspapers – women are weak, men are strong; if you're poor it's your own fault, people who are mentally ill are fundamentally flawed. More women, more blacks, more poor? Most psychiatrists are middle-class men as are most individuals with power in our society. Suddenly, the territory seemed (and seems still) very familiar.

Hospital Treatment
I investigated further afield visiting long-stay mental hospitals, community mental health centres and hostels. By and large, the regimes were friendly and modern with a similar analysis and approach. Labels were frowned upon, they weren't schizophrenics or psychotics, they were just people with problems; if there was better housing and more jobs, then less people would be coming through the doors. I started to become confused, what happened to the genetic defect, the chemical imbalance; I had been led to believe that they had an illness rather than problems. Also, arguing that unemployment and bad housing might be responsible for mental illness is a political statement. But the liberal stance is irrelevant given the brutality of some of the treatment; the medieval nature of electric shock treatment and the debilitating effect of some of the drug therapy.

One of the major classes of schizophrenia controlling drugs are the phenothiazenes. Unfortunately, long term use leads to incurable side effects: a shuffling gait, an inability to sit still for prolonged periods, problems with controlling the mouth, involuntary salivating and grunting. Certainly one of the major problems experienced by people who are diagnosed schizophrenic is that of having a very poor self-image, not least because of the economic and social situation they find themselves in. Indeed some would argue that a poor self-image is a necessary pre-condition to developing the illness in the first place. It would then seem, at the very least, unproductive to prescribe a drug whose long term side-effects are bound to diminish the patient's self-image even further for individuals thus afflicted are well aware of what they look like and how they sound.

In the end, what I discovered was simply more of the universal oppression of being diagnosed schizophrenic. The overriding inertia and hopelessness so prevalent in long-stay mental institutions began to affect me. I heard a number of stories from people who had been 'sectioned' against their will and I saw the lock-up wards. Once you are incarcerated in such a place, it is impossible to argue your sanity. To be quiet and accepting is to be withdrawn, to argue your case is to be disruptive; ultimately the justification for being there is that you are there. Similarly, it is claimed that no-one is forced to take medication but visiting relatives and friends are 'encouraged' to pressurise the inmates into accepting the 'treatment' with phrases like 'it's for your own good, the doctor says you'll be out quicker if you take your medicine'. Out quicker with a characteristic institution mentality, queuing for meals with a shuffling gait and gravy stained hospital suit.

Ordinary People
I read a number of books around the subject which suggested that all our perceptions are culturally constructed, that's why we find other cultures, other countries, strange, odd, bizarre. Most western civilisation can trace its philosophical ancestry back to the ancient Greeks and it was they who were responsible for introducing the notions of rationality and logic. Once they are accepted, the notion of madness is inevitable.

I thought again about the attitudes of the schizophrenics I knew; their reluctance to take their medication, their fear of returning to 'ward 39', their relentless, insistent need to forget their diagnosis, to be normal were all perfectly rational. Maybe, I concluded, I was wrong again about the writing workshop, it wasn't that they didn't want to unlock the door to themselves, they just wanted to escape their diagnosis and all it represented wherever and however it was manifested. I could hardly blame them, in their position, wouldn't anyone behave like that? Suddenly I was back at my arrogant starting point but for the wrong reasons. What did I say? 'In their position, wouldn't anyone behave like that?' But that's just another way of saying 'All mental illness is a rational response to the intolerable.'

THE PLAY

I set out to deal with the consequences of the illness rather than the illness itself and the play I produced is primarily about poverty. I enjoyed the writing. The research had taken over eight months and the actual placing of words on paper took just five weeks for the first draft. It was read and discussed. That draft did not contain the opportunity for actors to talk directly to the audience and given the expectations of *'Bruvvers'* audiences, that opportunity had to be there. Having written the first draft, I felt much more relaxed about solving this problem. It seemed important to me to stylise the audience contact in some way, it couldn't happen anywhere because the emotional moments in the play had to be achieved in order for it to work. I arrived at the idea of the actors speaking their own stage directions as a way of leading into the naturalism and out of it again. Within these stage directions it would be possible for contact to be established either by ad-libbing or simply by the way in which the speech was delivered. The idea was particularly appropriate because both the set and the characterisation were non-naturalistic. The set was a small rectangular stage with the audience seated on three sides and the band behind. Speaking their own stage directions meant that it was possible to say where the action was taking place and when with the minimum of props. The characterisation was helped because the acting company did not fit the ages of the characters. Thus it was possible for 34 year old Yvonne to say, 'I play Mary, she's around sixty...' and to become the character by adding bits of costume as the lines were said.

The rehearsal process was long, tiring and productive. It is not recommended for writers to direct their own work and in this case it was tough going. The major problem for the actors was understanding their extremely complex characters but ultimately this complexity proved a strength, it became stimulating. The whole process was collaborative and the actors (as always) contributed a great deal to the final text by discussing problems and suggesting and implementing changes. *Bruvvers* always have music in their productions and 'You've Got Me Singing The Blues' was written with the idea of accompanying it with blues music – hence the title. The idea was to give the oppression experienced by schizophrenics a broader perspective by setting it against the music produced by the american negroes from their suffering and difficulty. Two songs were written specially for the show by Rick

Stifter after a lot of discussion. These new songs were not blues; one was a spiritual and the other was a sad, slow number but they worked well with the other blues numbers and all the music dovetailed well into the show.

Steve Chambers
Heaton – March, 1988

Bruvvers Theatre Company

Bruvvers was founded in 1969 by Michael Mould, with the principle aim of taking theatre out to audiences who would not normally see any theatre. They tour mainly on Tyneside to community centres, schools, hospitals, youth clubs, etc.

However, Bruvvers have an international reputation, because of their stance on provision of theatre for working-class audiences, and their annual tour to Holland and Belgium.

Initially, Bruvvers were strongly supported by Northern Arts, but now they are funded by Newcastle City Council, who recognise the value of their work in combating disadvantage in the inner city area through (the application of) cultural events.

Bruvvers have produced over a hundred new plays; some written by company members, some written collectively by the company, and some written for them by local writers, amongst whom was C.P. Taylor.

Last year, Bruvvers were joint sponsors with Live Theatre (from October '86 to October '87) of the C.P. Taylor Bursary – a twelve-month bursary awarded to a local playwright, in this instance Steve Chambers, to work in the community in a way which is appropriate to the memory of Cecil. The final result of this support was 'You've Got Me Singing the Blues'. Bruvvers supported an extension of this by the Arts Council for a further six months, and also have commissioned Chambers' next play 'Tribal Pursuits', to be produced this autumn.

Michael Mould – June 1988

Live Theatre Co.

Formed by a group of Tyneside actors in the early 'Seventies, Live Theatre's main aim is to tour relevant and entertaining productions to the non-theatre venues in the North East. In the absence of suitable scripts, the company initially devised its own shows but in 1975 began to work with the North Shields-based playwright, Tom Hadaway, and from that time onwards became committed to the development of Northern "new writing". Their long partnership with C.P. Taylor produced outstanding plays for both young people and for adults, including "Operation Elvis", "A Nightingale Sang" and "The Saints Come Marching In".

Their sponsorship of Steve Chambers for the C.P. Taylor Bursary and indeed their current programme of new writing reflects their continuing commitment to exciting new work for working class audiences in the region.

Dave Clarke – August 1988

Production Notes

The convention of actors talking to the audience is encouraged in the production of this play. The main device to enable this to happen is that the actors speak their own stage directions and occasionally converse with the audience. It is at these defined points that audience contact is created and maintained. I didn't want to use the device of 'talking to the audience' alone because I felt that that would make the transition from actor to character more difficult both for the audience and the actors. A great number of the scenes are highly emotional and I think that actors must engage in their own research before they can attempt to play these characters. The stage directions are thus an intermediate stage between direct audience contact and playing a role.

I have adopted the convention in the script of italicizing lines which are spoken by the actor as opposed to the character although all lines will be denoted by the character name.

In the first production, blues music was played by the company. The songs used were:

'Nobody Knows You When You're Down and Out' to begin the play.

A spiritual written by the company for Christine at the end of Scene 2.

'Bricks in My Pillow' – an original blues number at the end of Scene 3.

'Help Me' at the end of Scene 4.

A specially written song at the end Scene 5.

'Buddy Can You Spare a Dime' at the end of Scene 6.

'Trouble in Mind' begun by Bobby on the harmonica at the end of the play.

Obviously, the music could be a sound tape or played or something else but the play was designed to be accompanied by blues music.

YOU'VE GOT ME SINGING THE BLUES

This play was first performed by BRUVVERS Theatre Co. at Live Theatre, Newcastle on Tyne, on October 12th, 1987. The cast list (with ages of the characters) was as follows:

BOBBY (40)	–	*BILL SPEED*
GEORGE (55)	–	*MICHAEL MOULD*
MARY (60)	–	*YVONNE KINGSWELL*
STUART (28)	–	*STEVE THIRKELD*
COLIN-DOUGLAS (38)	–	*RICK STIFTER*
CHRISTINE (34)	–	*LIBBY DAVISON*

●

DIRECTOR	–	*STEVE CHAMBERS*
DESIGNER	–	*MICHAEL MOULD*
MUSICAL DIRECTOR	–	*RICK STIFTER*

You've Got Me Singing The Blues

Act One

Scene One

THE PLAY OPENS WITH THE COMPANY SINGING A BLUES NUMBER (THE SONG OF THE SHOW?). AT THE END OF THE SONG, BOBBY APPEARS FROM THE AUDIENCE AND BEGINS PLAYING THE HARMONICA AS IF HE IS A BUSKER OFF THE STREET WHO HAS GOT INTO THE THEATRE BY ACCIDENT. HE ASKS FOR MONEY. THE REST OF THE COMPANY TRY TO DEAL WITH HIM, ASKING HIM TO LEAVE, TELLING HIM THEY'VE GOT A SHOW TO DO.

BOBBY   Hey that was great... (*PUTS CAP DOWN ON THE FLOOR*) Here listen to this one... (*PLAYS HARMONICA... THE REST OF THE CAST TRY TO DEAL WITH HIM*)

OTHERS   Come on... we've got a show to do...

BOBBY   Hey... you've had your go... GERROFF... HEY... WHO'RE YOU SHOVING... (*FIGHTING BACK*) GET OFF ME... WHAT'S UP... DON'T YOU LIKE MUSIC EH? TOERAGS!...STUFF YOU!
That was Bobby, That's who I play in this story... you'll have seen him down on the quayside or up Northumberland Street busking He lives in this house with these other blokes who you'll meet later. All the people in this play are diagnosed schizophrenics... Anyway, Bobby's gone up Northumberland Street... to do a bit of busking...
(*PLAYS THE HARMONICA*) HEY... DON'T YOU LIKE MUSIC... TOERAGS...
Bad day for busking... bloody Sundays...
(*PLAYS SOME MORE*) I try other days... I'm fed up today though.
Have to be careful or I'll end up with the blues... I don't get them you know but I get close some Sundays like... still you can get along Northumberland Street and see what's in the shops... take your time... hah hah...

plenty of time... I'm not short of that...
(ENTER GEORGE)

GEORGE | *He turns to a character George.*

BOBBY | Aye aye George.

GEORGE | Alright? (*BOBBY NODS*) George, that's who I play, well he's fifty-five, ex-welder, ex-member of the communist party. He's been taking these drugs, phenothiazenes for years and they've left him with a shuffling gait (*SHUFFLES*) an inability to sit still. (*HE SITS DOWN AND STANDS UP DURING THE NEXT BIT*) He feels the need to to stand up and sit down again during conversations, He has trouble controlling his mouth. (*HE OPENS AND CLOSES IT AND ROLLS HIS TONGUE AROUND TO DEMONSTRATE.*) Sometimes, he grunts involuntarily as he breathes. He knows its going on and that it bothers people but what can he do? He's become a spectator of his own body's needs. Now this play starts on a Sunday and ends on a Wednesday of the same week. George, that's me, he's one of the blokes who lives with Bobby and this conversation took place a little earlier in the house.

BOBBY | You should come along George... the fresh air would do you good...

GEORGE | (*SITTING*) I'm not well man... haven't had my injection... my heart and that...

BOBBY | Come and watch me busk eh? Good music, fresh air... better than sitting inside... see some women eh... hah hah... (*BOTH LAUGH*)...that'd cheer you up... all dressed up in their Sunday best... hah hah... ooh eh!

GEORGE | Aye... I've been hearing my voices again... I don't want to tell the psychiatrist because he'll put me back in hospital... what do you think I should do Bobby?

You've Got Me Singing The Blues

BOBBY　　　　Don't know...

GEORGE　　　I'll have to sort it out otherwise it'll be the eight men in white coats from Jubilee Road again... (*SINGS*) 'They're coming to take me away hah hah...' (*BOTH LAUGH*)

BOBBY　　　　You should take your injection... then you wouldn't hear the voices...

GEORGE　　　I think you've got to tell the psychiatrist the truth... no point in lying... I'll say its spirits not voices... (*PAUSE*)...I don't know whether to walk to the hospital or get the bus...

BOBBY　　　　You should come for a walk with me man... do you good...

GEORGE　　　No... I haven't got the energy... (*STANDS UP AND LOOKS AROUND FLEXING HIS ARMS LIMPLY, THEN SITS AGAIN*) my muscles are all to hell since they changed my injection... you're on depixel aren't you?

BOBBY　　　　Depixel aye...

GEORGE　　　I used to be on that... should have left me on it... this stuff they're giving me now... that's the problem... should never have changed it... (*PAUSE*)
I think I'll get the bus there and walk back... what do you think?

BOBBY　　　　You're not coming then? (*GEORGE SHAKES HIS HEAD AND EXITS*) *Well he didn't come so Bobby went up Northumberland Street.* I walk everywhere... it's cheaper. Sundays... sometimes I go over to the Cyreneans on Westgate Road for my dinner... but I didn't today. The Wayside club opens at 2 and I have a cup of tea in there... one of them drop-in centres... all sitting round the walls like zombies or I might go to the Catholic Listening Post for a change... and then I'm off again... hah hah... I don't hang about me... down

17

Steve Chambers

	Northumberland Street, do a bit of busking and then drift towards the station, see what the crowd's like... do a bit more... and then by about 4 I'm down here, on the quayside under the Tyne Bridge, sit and watch the boats... and the gulls eh... (*SITS DOWN, TAKES OFF HAVERSACK, TAKES FLASK OUT OF THE HAVERSACK AND POURS HIMSELF SOME TEA, ROLLS HIMSELF A CIGARETTE*) I don't drink now... not me... some do like... (*TAKES SIP FROM FLASK*) Tea, that's my liquor... hah hah... I don't buy milk either... too expensive... yeah that's it... powdered milk's cheaper... I make up half a pint a day... well some days I can't be bothered... (*ENTER MARY*)
MARY	Who're you talking to son... eh? *Enter Mary, she is a woman of around sixty... sixty-one to be precise... that's who I play. She lives alone... and she's cantankerous... always thinks people are getting at her... well a lot of the time they are.* Who're you talking to son eh?
BOBBY	What? Oh hello Mary...
MARY	Howay then, give us a kiss... (*BOBBY DOES SO*) I thought I'd find you down here...
BOBBY	Aye... (*MARY TAKES BOBBY'S CUP AND POURS HERSELF A CUP FROM BOBBY'S FLASK*) Want some tea?
MARY	Where's the others then?
BOBBY	Don't know...
MARY	I went round the house and there was no answer... there's always someone there on a Sunday...
BOBBY	George isn't well... (*BEGINS TO PLAY HARMONICA AGAIN*)
MARY	(*TAKES A SIP OF THE TEA AND SPITS IT OUT*) This

	is horrible… what did you put in it?
BOBBY	(TAKING IT OFF HER) You don't have to drink it… Don't you take sugar then?
MARY	It's the milk… it's off… you're trying to poison me!
BOBBY	It's powdered milk… it's cheaper, that's all…
MARY	It's bloody awful… (PAUSE) Are you sure you're not trying to poison me… eh?
BOBBY	I'm drinking it aren't I? (HE IGNORES HER AND BEGINS TO ROLL ANOTHER CIGARETTE… SHE WATCHES HIM)
MARY	What's wrong with George then?
BOBBY	Hasn't had his injection… he's worried they'll put him back in the hospital…
MARY	You get decent grub in there… (PAUSE) I was coming round for my tea… my cats are starving… they need feeding…
BOBBY	We've got nothing for ourselves…
MARY	What about my cats then?
BOBBY	Don't know…
MARY	My cats will starve and you don't care… (BEGINS TO SOB)…you don't care…
BOBBY	Cats man… they can look after themselves, they'll be alright… (MARY SOBS LOUDLY). Look we haven't got anything… the shops will be open tomorrow… you can get some scraps then…
MARY	They're hungry now… and there's a kitten, Bobby I've called him… he can't look after himself… (SOBS TO HERSELF)

BOBBY   You should have gone to St. Thomas's... good grub there...

MARY   I went last week... didn't like it... all those men bloody swearing... (SOBS)

BOBBY   Hey... hah hah... guess where I had breakfast this morning? Come on guess... (SHE DOESN'T ANSWER) Grey Street... hah hah...

MARY   Where did you get the money?

BOBBY   Money... hah hah... I didn't need any... I stood in the street with the traffic going past and ate my sandwiches... get it... I had my breakfast in Grey street... (HE LAUGHS LOUDLY)

MARY   I hate Sundays... there's no one to talk to...

BOBBY   That's the one thing I like about them... talking's over rated if you ask me.

MARY   I like to talk... I thought Stuart might be in, he likes talking...

BOBBY   He does and all... mind, that's all they did in the hospital... talk... never helped me...

MARY   Stuart likes his Sundays.

BOBBY   Aye... He's gone with Colin-Douglas to see Christine in St Nick's...

MARY   That's still going on is it?

BOBBY   Hah hah... never stops... they'll be cadging their tea in the hospital... we're all broke by Sunday so there's not a lot of choice... not a lot of choice anyway if you've got no money... (STANDS UP AND BUTTONS UP HIS COAT, PACKS HIS HAVERSACK AND PUTS IT ON HIS BACK... PUTS HIS CAP ON)

MARY   What are you doing?

BOBBY	Going...
MARY	You're not leaving me are you?
BOBBY	No...
MARY	You were... you were going to leave me...
BOBBY	I'd better get back and see how George is... You can come with me... I'll make you a cup of tea when we get back...
MARY	Not with that horrible milk you won't...
BOBBY	We might have some ordinary...
MARY	Buy some...
BOBBY	I haven't got any money left...
MARY	I bet you've got some...
BOBBY	You buy the milk if its that important to you!
MARY	You don't like me now do you?...
BOBBY	(BOBBY GOES TO GO THEN STOPS) Come on. (EXITS)
MARY	Will you give me some scraps for the cats... they're hungry... (FOLLOWS BOBBY, EXITS)

Scene Two
AN ORGAN PLAYS CHAPEL OF REST MUSIC QUIETLY DURING THIS SCENE

GEORGE It's Sunday afternoon and this is Colin–Douglas ... say hello...

COLIN-DOUGLAS Hello...

STUART He's a tory... well he doesn't know any better... I'm Stuart... and me and Colin live with Bobby and George...

GEORGE Stuart... he's a bit younger than the rest of us and he's a bit of a clever shite... anyway, they've come to visit Christine... we are in the church in St Nick's mental hospital. There is a man with a microphone... (TAKES MIKE)...and I'll play him for this scene... he works in the hospital... (TO AUDIENCE) You're part of the congregation right... that's it... show the proper respect and something else? Oh yes Colin-Douglas and Stuart are arguing.

MAN Fellow Christians let us contemplate in our own minds the goodness of God... and as we reflect in this brief moment of quiet, let us remember all those less fortunate than ourselves... (THE REST BOW THEIR HEADS, STUART LOOKS AROUND)

STUART Less fortunate than ourselves... that's a good one...

COLIN-DOUGLAS SSh...

STUART I shouldn't have come...

COLIN-DOUGLAS Christine wanted us to... anyway, I think people should go to church on Sundays...

STUART Why?

COLIN-DOUGLAS It's good for the soul...

STUART	What does that mean?
COLIN-DOUGLAS	Everybody needs to believe in something, it's natural...
VOICE	Ssh!
STUART	Look, half the people in here (*GESTURING TO AUDIENCE*) have been locked up for seeing God or hearing His voice... then when they put you in here, they make you go along and pretend you can hear the word of God... but if you do hear Him, they bang you back in the lock-up ward... it's stupid...
COLIN-DOUGLAS	You're being ridiculous...
STUART	Religion can't help people and certainly not those who are mentally ill... you should know that...
COLIN-DOUGLAS	I'm not mentally ill...
STUART	You were...
COLIN-DOUGLAS	Well, I'm not now... I never heard any voices...
STUART	I did... I still do from time to time... But I don't believe in religion... I never have... Take the Pope... he dresses up in a fancy white dress and whenever he lands in a foreign country he kisses the tarmac...
COLIN-DOUGLAS	That's tradition...
STUART	If you or I put on a white dress in Northumberland Street and stop the traffic so we can kiss the road, we'd be back in here straight away...
COLIN-DOUGLAS	Well you'd better not let Christine hear you say that...
CHRISTINE	(*CHRISTINE ENTERS FROM THE BACK*) What

mustn't I hear? (*THEY STOP AND LOOK AT HER*) *I play Christine... She's 28 and she lives in the hospital but gets out every other day... she's not very well...* (CHRISTINE COMES OVER TO THEM)
Hello my two darlings... what mustn't I hear? (*SHE KISSES COLIN–DOUGLAS FORCEFULLY ON THE LIPS AND STUART LOOKS PISSED OFF. SHE FINISHES AND COLIN–DOUGLAS LOOKS TRIUMPHANTLY AT STUART*)

COLIN-DOUGLAS   Stuart was being blasphemous weren't you?

STUART   No... you can't be blasphemous about something you don't believe in... (*HE BEGINS TO SPEAK WHEN CHRISTINE KISSES HIM PASSIONATELY ON THE LIPS AND COLIN–DOUGLAS LOOKS ANGRY AND FED UP*)

CHRISTINE   My Stuart wouldn't do that now would you? (TO COLIN–DOUGLAS) You shouldn't go spreading naughty rumours... God will punish you... He doesn't like nastiness...

COLIN-DOUGLAS   I wasn't spreading rumours...

VOICE   SSH!

CHRISTINE   Now let's go and pray together...

STUART   I don't want to...

CHRISTINE   To be covered in the blood of the lamb of God... (*SHE TAKES THE ARM OF STUART AND LEADS HIM AWAY FROM COLIN–DOUGLAS*) Come on Colin–Douglas... there's no need to sulk...

STUART   That's right Colin... you mustn't sulk...

COLIN-DOUGLAS   I wasn't... (*THE MAN ON THE MICROPHONE BEGINS TO SPEAK*)

MAN   Ladies and gentlemen... we have come together in the sight of God... let us pray...

You've Got Me Singing The Blues

(CHRISTINE BOWS HER HEAD OSTENTATIOUSLY... COLIN–DOUGLAS SCOWLS AT STUART WHO GRIMACES BACK... CHRISTINE SEES THEM AND NUDGES THEM... COLIN–DOUGLAS BOWS HIS HEAD AND SO DOES STUART WHO THEN CONTINUES DIGGING COLIN–DOUGLAS IN THE BACK DURING THE PRAYING) Oh God we beseech You to come into our hearts and minds and to grant us salvation... help us to find peace especially the tormented souls on this earthly plane... (AT THIS POINT COLIN–DOUGLAS RETALIATES AND PUSHES STUART BACK)

STUART Hey what're you doing?

COLIN-DOUGLAS Get off...

CHRISTINE Stop it... in the house of God...

MAN We live in troubled times... but we must strive to repent of our sins...

STUART Crap!

COLIN-DOUGLAS There you heard... he blasphemed...

CHRISTINE We must pray for him...

COLIN-DOUGLAS I'm not...

STUART I don't need your prayers...

CHRISTINE SSh!

MAN The Lord is bountiful in His wisdom and forgiveness...

CHRISTINE He is... Amen to that... I want Him to come and take me... maybe if we pray, He'll call us together...

STUART He won't call me...

COLIN-DOUGLAS You're right there...

STUART	Well He won't be calling you either...
COLIN-DOUGLAS	Oh aye?
STUART	He doesn't wear a pin-stripe suit and vote tory you know...
COLIN-DOUGLAS	Look, He wouldn't take a waster like you... blaspheming and drinking and scrounging your way through life...
CHRISTINE	I want Him to call me... oh please Jesus...
STUART	Well, you're not a proper tory, you live in Walker... He only takes tories who live in Ponteland...
CHRISTINE	Ssh let us pray together...
MAN	And finally Lord let us ask for Your blessing on those who dwell for the time being in this hospital. Grant us Your forgiveness and help us to see the light of Your presence and help us out of our darkness... Amen.
CHRISTINE	Amen!...Oh I wish He'd take me...
COLIN-DOUGLAS	I don't want Him to take you...
CHRISTINE	Oh you are sweet... all the men in here fancy me you know... but I tell them I've got my boyfriends... Stuart (*KISSES HIM*) and Colin-Douglas... (*KISSES HIM*)
STUART	Can we go yet?
CHRISTINE	No! I'm singing now...
MAN	And now the first hymn is going to be sung for us by Christine... Christine?
CHRISTINE	I'm here... (*TO COLIN–DOUGLAS AND STUART*) Now you stay and listen... (*GOES TO THE MICROPHONE*)

You've Got Me Singing The Blues

COLIN-DOUGLAS   (TO STUART) You go if you want...

STUART   No I'll stay... Christine likes me...

COLIN-DOUGLAS   She likes me better...

STUART   Like hell she does.

COLIN-DOUGLAS   We're going away together...

STUART   You're not...

COLIN-DOUGLAS   Ask her if you don't believe me...

STUART   I will (DURING THIS CONVERSATION, CHRISTINE HAS BEEN GETTING READY TO SING HER HYMN... SHE HAS BEGUN THE FIRST LINE OF THE HYMN WHEN STUART INTERRUPTS)

STUART   Christine.

CHRISTINE   I'm singing...

MAN   Won't you sit down?

STUART   Christine are you going away with Colin-Douglas?

MAN   Please?

STUART   ARE YOU?

CHRISTINE   Yes... isn't that lovely... me and Colin together...

STUART   You won't... (MARCHES OFF)

COLIN-DOUGLAS   (TO STUART AS HE LEAVES) See?

CHRISTINE   Don't go Stuart... (STUART EXITS) I wanted him to hear me sing... (SHE BEGINS TO SING A HYMN WHICH IS ALSO A NEGRO SPIRITUAL WHICH THEN BECOMES A BLUES NUMBER).

Steve Chambers

Scene Three

GEORGE	*It's Monday morning now and this is the living-room of the house shared by George, Colin-Douglas, Stuart and Bobby.* (ENTER MARY)
MARY	*Mary's asleep in a chair with a blanket round her* (SITS DOWN AND PUTS BLANKET ROUND HER)
GEORGE	(SITTING DOWN WITH A SHEET) *Bobby is in the kitchen* (ENTER BOBBY) *George who is not very well is asleep on another chair.* (GEORGE SLEEPS)
BOBBY	I'm preparing my flask for the day. (DOES SO) *Colin-Douglas enters with a suitcase.*
COLIN-DOUGLAS	Well… that's me… I'm all set… hey you know, I reckon… (BOBBY LEAVES THE KITCHEN)
BOBBY	SSh!…Keep your voice down… Mary and George… (COLIN-DOUGLAS FROWNS AND SEES THEM) He's getting worse and I don't think Mary's that grand…
COLIN-DOUGLAS	She's well enough to get round here every Sunday afternoon when she's run out of what she's got. (BOBBY RETURNS TO THE KITCHEN AND CARRIES ON GETTING READY)
COLIN-DOUGLAS	Hey… I reckon there might be some work you know…
BOBBY	I'm going up the Wellfield today… see what I can get…
COLIN-DOUGLAS	No man… in London… London's a big place and the unemployment's not so bad down there…
BOBBY	London?
COLIN-DOUGLAS	Yeah…

You've Got Me Singing The Blues

BOBBY   When are you going then?

COLIN-DOUGLAS   Tonight.

BOBBY   Not long eh?

COLIN-DOUGLAS   Hah hah... I'm off... (*HOLDS UP CASE*) I've got my things and I'll be off (*AS THEY ARE TALKING GEORGE HAS WOKEN UP... HE SEES MARY ASLEEP, GOES OVER TO HER AND LOOKS CLOSELY AT HER.*)

BOBBY   (*PACKING HIS THERMOS FLASK AND OTHER THINGS INTO HIS HAVERSACK*) I'll see you before you go then... tonight?

COLIN-DOUGLAS   Should do... (*AT THIS MOMENT MARY WAKES UP AND SCREAMS BECAUSE GEORGE IS KISSING HER... COLIN-DOUGLAS AND BOBBY GO INTO THE ROOM TO SEE WHAT IS HAPPENING*)

MARY   Get off me! (*SLAPS HIM*) You dirty old bugger...

GEORGE   You hit me...

MARY   I'll do a bit more than hit you... (*GOING AFTER HIM... GEORGE RETREATS AND HIDES BEHIND COLIN*)...Come here you old bugger...

COLIN-DOUGLAS   (*TO MARY*) Sit down and calm down...

GEORGE   She's gone mad...

MARY   That's good coming from you...

BOBBY   What's happened?

MARY   He attacked me when I was asleep... dirty bugger...

GEORGE   I just gave a her a kiss... that's all...

MARY   Aye, that's all... but only because I woke up...

GEORGE | I'm not well you know... (*SITTING DOWN*)...

COLIN-DOUGLAS | (*TO MARY*) You shouldn't be here... you don't pay any rent...

MARY | Neither do you... the social pay it for you...

COLIN-DOUGLAS | It's our house...

MARY | You don't want me then... nobody wants me... (*BEGINS TO SOB*)

GEORGE | I think I'll have a wash... (*GEORGE GETS UP AND GOES TO WHERE THE KITCHEN WAS AND MIMES WASHING WHILE MARY SOBS WITH RENEWED VIGOUR*)

BOBBY | You've started her off...

COLIN-DOUGLAS | What did I do? She shouldn't stay the night... it's not proper... (*MARY WEEPS LOUDLY AS STUART ENTERS HOLDING A PAPER BAG ALOFT LIKE A TROPHY*)

STUART | They're still there! I have proof! (*MARY CONTINUES CRYING, STUART SEES HER*) What's the matter now?

MARY | No-one likes me...

BOBBY | We do...

GEORGE | I do...

MARY | (*BRIGHTENING UP*) Oh I know what you like you old bugger...

STUART | Right well gather round and listen to me... you too Colin... As I said... I now have absolute proof that we have rats living in our yard...

BOBBY | What's in the bag?

STUART | Evidence... they'll have to do something

You've Got Me Singing The Blues

COLIN-DOUGLAS They'll probably put you back in Ward 39...

STUART Well, I'd be close to Christine then, wouldn't I?

BOBBY It's not rats man... it's dogs...

STUART I know the noise a rat makes... you know I don't sleep... I hear them scurrying around... spreading disease... the council will have to do something about it...

BOBBY I still think it's dogs...

STUART I've got proof!

COLIN-DOUGLAS What is it then?

STUART (PUTS BAG IN HIS POCKET) You'll find out when the time comes...

BOBBY Oh suit yourself... I'm off to the Wellfield... (PUTS HAVERSACK ON HIS BACK)

STUART Hey Bobby, you're wasting your time going to that place... it's slave labour...

BOBBY Maybe...

COLIN-DOUGLAS How would you know?... you've never done a days work in your life...

STUART I did that job scraping graffiti off school desks for three months... that's where I met Christine... at least there we got decent wages... not like the Wellfield... a weeks work for seven quid... It's a punishment for being diagnosed... tell them to stuff it...

COLIN-DOUGLAS We have to show willing... they'll help those who help themselves...

STUART You'll believe anything they tell you won't

	you?
BOBBY	I'm going... alright! (TO COLIN) See you before you go...
COLIN-DOUGLAS	Yep... yep... hah... hah... (BOBBY EXITS)
MARY	Don't leave me Bobby son... don't leave me... (GOES AFTER HIM... EXITS)
GEORGE	(GEORGE RETURNS FROM THE KITCHEN DRYING HIMSELF) Well you certainly started something today Colin... it'll just be you and me soon Stuart.
STUART	How do you mean?
GEORGE	Colin... he's getting a job in London... well aren't you?
COLIN-DOUGLAS	How do you know?
GEORGE	I overheard...
COLIN-DOUGLAS	I thought you were asleep...
GEORGE	I was close to the surface like... I thought it was some of my voices so I listened without moving...
COLIN-DOUGLAS	You should sleep in your own bedroom... in a bed... then you might be able to sleep properly... I bet your social worker doesn't know you're sleeping down here...
STUART	Stuff the bloody social worker... what's it got to do with them where he sleeps?
COLIN-DOUGLAS	I don't think it's right...
GEORGE	They don't need to know Colin man... it's just... well... I can't be bothered at the moment... my bedroom needs tidying and I can't face it... when I pull myself round, I'll sort it out... but I've got a bad heart and those

	stairs...
STUART	Don't let him get at you George... I bet his social worker doesn't know he's off to London... but... he's like most tories... only cares about himself...
COLIN-DOUGLAS	(*BRANDISHING HIS SUITCASE*) You'll see... at least I'm doing something...
GEORGE	Big place London... lots of dossers...
STUART	There'll be one more soon...
COLIN-DOUGLAS	I'll find somewhere to live...
GEORGE	When he's got a job... that's it eh Colin?
STUART	And what job could you do?
COLIN-DOUGLAS	There's lots of jobs I could do... you read about people becoming overnight successes... why shouldn't it happen to me eh?
STUART	As soon as an employer finds you're a schizophrenic, you'll be out on your ear...
COLIN-DOUGLAS	How are they going to find out? I'm not going to tell them...
STUART	You'll get ill...
GEORGE	It's the stress man... gets to you... people shouting at you and telling you off... and you'll be lonely on your own there...
COLIN-DOUGLAS	I shan't be alone... Christine is coming with me... (*LOOKS AT STUART AND BEGINS TO LAUGH*) Yep... yep... she is... see...
STUART	They'll never let her out of St. Nicks...
COLIN-DOUGLAS	It's all arranged...
STUART	I'll tell the hospital...

Steve Chambers

GEORGE · You'd better be quick, they're going tonight... that's right isn't it? (SPENDS THE REST OF THE SCENE LOOKING FOR AN OVERCOAT)

STUART · (STUART GETTING READY TO GO) I'm going up there to see her...

COLIN-DOUGLAS · Don't you go upsetting her...

STUART · She's not well...

COLIN-DOUGLAS · You're jealous... you told me that she should be allowed out all the time...

STUART · But not with you! (EXITS)

GEORGE · Terrible thing... jealousy... mind, she's a good looking woman...

COLIN-DOUGLAS · He'd better not upset her...

GEORGE · I'm going to the hospital today... you couldn't lend me the bus-fare could you?

COLIN-DOUGLAS · Look, I need everything I've got to go to London...

GEORGE · Do you think I should tell the psychiatrist I've been hearing my voices again?

COLIN-DOUGLAS · You should have your injection... do as you're told...

GEORGE · I don't trust them... doctors... they're from the bosses class...

COLIN-DOUGLAS · They know what's best... they're trained... we won't get better if we don't take our medicine...

GEORGE · We don't seem to get any better...

COLIN-DOUGLAS · If you think like that you won't... it's a long haul... but you've got to take risks... like me going to London...

GEORGE	Yeah... you've got to take each day as it comes... write down what you're going to do each day and then do it... that's right isn't it?
COLIN-DOUGLAS	I'm going up there... I'll stop him... she'll come... (*EXITS*)
GEORGE	I'll sort out my room when I get on my feet... Take each day as it comes... I wonder if I should get the bus... they say walking's good for the heart, I hope it doesn't rain... I'm too old to go back in there... it's full of weirdos and I can't cope with the violent ones... I think I'll get the bus to the hospital and walk back... (*DURING THIS SPEECH, THE BEGINNING INSTRUMENTAL ACCOMPANIMENT OF A SONG PLAYS UNDER IT. GEORGE MAKES SPEECH AS HE GOES INTO THE BAND.*)

Scene Four

BOBBY	*It's still Monday and Bobby's visiting Christine at the hospital. She's got a carrier bag.* (ENTER CHRISTINE WITH A CARRIER BAG) So how are you?
CHRISTINE	Alright Bobby… they're letting me out soon you know…
BOBBY	Yeah? I think George will be coming back…
CHRISTINE	Poor George…
BOBBY	He's been hearing his voices again… he hasn't had his injection…
CHRISTINE	Maybe he'll hear God's voice…
BOBBY	Aye…
CHRISTINE	I wish God would speak to me… and then take me.
BOBBY	When are they letting you out then?
CHRISTINE	Today…
BOBBY	Today… well where's your stuff?
CHRISTINE	I've got it here… (HOLDING UP THE BAG)
BOBBY	There's not much there is there…?
CHRISTINE	I don't need much…
BOBBY	You must have more than that though… if you leave it behind, it'll just go into the hospital fund… when you come back, you'll see someone else wearing your gear… you don't want that…
CHRISTINE	You are sweet Bobby…

BOBBY   Aye...

CHRISTINE   My sweet Bobby...

BOBBY   Where will you live?

CHRISTINE   Somewhere nice where we can be together...

BOBBY   Who's that with then? Colin?

CHRISTINE   No, my children... Robert Shaun, Paul Patrick and Loraine Marie...

BOBBY   I didn't know you had children Christine...

CHRISTINE   Oh yes... Robert Shaun was born on the twelfth of September, 1976 and he weighed eight pounds seven ounces... imagine that... he was a big baby with jet black hair and he cried all the time till he had his nipple... men are like that... cry till they've had their nipple... and Paul Patrick was a lovely baby... quiet, good natured......he had jaundice, poor thing... all yellow... he and Robert Shaun used to play together as toddlers... I had them close together... an accident...

BOBBY   Were you married then?

CHRISTINE   I still am but now it's to Jesus... sweet baby Jesus...

BOBBY   I've never been married...

CHRISTINE   A lovely man like you... that's a shame...

BOBBY   I've known women like... hah hah... I've known women alright... love them and leave them eh? That's the way...

CHRISTINE   My man left me... then I got ill...

BOBBY   Where are the bairns then?

CHRISTINE   They took them off us... when I was ill...

	they won't tell me where they are... but I'm going to find them... Jesus will help me... He wouldn't want me not to see my darlings would He? It's Loraine Marie's birthday tomorrow... (TAKES A PRESENT FROM HER BAG)...she'll be eight... (BOBBY LOOKS CONFUSED) It's her present; she must have a present from her mother on her birthday...
BOBBY	(EXAMINING A BARBIE DOLL) That's nice... she'll like that but what's the point if you don't know where she is...
CHRISTINE	I'll find her one day won't I? I'll find all three and then they can have the presents I've got them... Christmas and birthdays... what a day that will be for them... their little faces smiling... all that love from their mother... (PAUSE) I don't know whether they've been kept together... I hope so... I like to think of them playing together... (PAUSE) I might find them in London...
BOBBY	Colin's going to London...
CHRISTINE	Colin-Douglas, he's nice... have you got a middle name Bobby?
BOBBY	No... not me... just plain Robert... Bobby...
CHRISTINE	It's a nice name... suits you... you couldn't be anything else I don't think... (ENTER STUART)
STUART	This is cosy... you're chatting her up now are you?
BOBBY	What?
STUART	You and Christine...
CHRISTINE	He's just come to see me darling...
STUART	I can see that...

BOBBY	I often do it…
STUART	Oh do you… I thought you were going to the Wellfield…
BOBBY	I went… they hadn't got anything… well they were full up… maybe in a year's time…
STUART	A year's time… you mean they're queuing up to be slaves now are they?
CHRISTINE	Stuart, you don't have to shout… God can hear you perfectly well if you speak calmly… He hears everything we utter, He knows every thought we have…
STUART	Christine, can I talk to you… on our own?
BOBBY	I'll go… (GETTING UP)
CHRISTINE	No… stay… (TO STUART) Bobby's been nice to me… we've been talking haven't we? (STUART BEGINS TO SAY SOMETHING) And he's your friend too… we should be friends together.
STUART	Christine, Colin says you and him are off to London tonight… is that right?
CHRISTINE	Yes… that's nice isn't it?
STUART	It's a bad idea…
CHRISTINE	Jesus loves us all you know… you have to let Him into your heart…
STUART	I'm not worried about letting Jesus into your heart, it's letting Colin in that bothers me… I mean, what's he got that I haven't eh? Is he better looking? Is he cleverer? Is he more interesting to talk to? (TO BOBBY) He's not is he? He's a boring tory… believes everything he's told… well it's true isn't it… You know what I mean don't you Bob? (BOBBY DOESN'T ANSWER) I just don't understand what you see

	in him...
CHRISTINE	I like you both... (KISSING STUART, SEES BOBBY LOOKING) Don't feel left out... (KISSING BOBBY) I like you too... you're lovely...
STUART	I'll take you to Edinburgh... Edinburgh's much nicer than London...
CHRISTINE	No, they're not in Scotland... they might be in the Midlands though... I think someone told me that... or did I dream it... I can't remember.
STUART	You can't just walk out of here... they won't let you go...
CHRISTINE	They know... they don't mind... (ENTER COLIN–DOUGLAS)
COLIN-DOUGLAS	Christine, is he bothering you?
STUART	No I'm not...
BOBBY	I'll go... (GETTING UP)
COLIN-DOUGLAS	No you stay, I want you as a witness... (BOBBY SITS AGAIN)
STUART	What to? A murder...?
COLIN-DOUGLAS	(TO CHRISTINE) Are you ready then?
CHRISTINE	Yes... I have my things... Oh I am looking forward to seeing the sights... can we go in the cathedrals... they have wonderful ones in London...
COLIN-DOUGLAS	Yes... I'll take you to Westminster Abbey and St. Paul's...
STUART	They're no good... (COLIN–DOUGLAS LOOKS BLANK) Christine's a Catholic... you'll need to find a Catholic cathedral... (TO CHRISTINE) See Christine, you should stay here and let me

	take you somewhere, he doesn't understand you like I do…
COLIN-DOUGLAS	At least I'm a Christian, you're a bloody heathen… unbeliever, unbeliever, hey… yeah?
STUART	You aren't a Christian… you're a tory… you can't be both.(ENTER GEORGE AND MARY, GEORGE HAS AN ENVELOPE IN HIS HAND)
MARY	There they are… I told you they'd be here…
GEORGE	There's Bobby, I thought you were going to the Wellfield…
BOBBY	I've been… (GETS UP TO GO)
MARY	What's wrong son? You're not leaving because I've come are you?
BOBBY	No, I've heard enough shouting for today… that's all…
GEORGE	You should stay…
BOBBY	Why?
GEORGE	To hear this… (HOLDING UP THE LETTER, BOBBY TAKES THE LETTER OUT OF THE ENVELOPE AND READS IT AS…) Hello Christine, you're looking well…
CHRISTINE	Hello George… Mary… I'm going away…
COLIN-DOUGLAS	(TO CHRISTINE) Come on… we'll go… (SHE GATHERS HER BAG)
GEORGE	Don't I get a kiss before you go?
MARY	Don't start George…
STUART	(TO COLIN–DOUGLAS) You're not going…
COLIN-DOUGLAS	Yep… yep… we are… (TAKES CHRISTINE BY

THE ARM AND STARTS TO LEAD HER AWAY)

BOBBY   The rent hasn't been paid... they're going to evict us next Monday.

GEORGE   I paid my share... what does it mean?

COLIN-DOUGLAS   The rent hasn't been paid?

BOBBY   That's what it says... (*HANDS LETTER TO COLIN–DOUGLAS WHO READS IT*)

STUART   They don't mean it...

COLIN-DOUGLAS   They do... my God... what will we do?

CHRISTINE   Aren't we going now Colin-Douglas?

COLIN-DOUGLAS   In a minute Christine...

STUART   I told you you wouldn't go...

GEORGE   Is it because the house is untidy?

BOBBY   The rent's not been paid man...

GEORGE   Well Stuart pays the rent... they must have made a mistake... (*SITTING AND HOLDING HIS HEAD*) I'd better see the psychiatrist... (*STANDS AGAIN*) I need my injection... (*BOBBY AND COLIN–DOUGLAS LOOK AT STUART*)

MARY   He's not there... you've got to wait until four o'clock...

GEORGE   (*TALKING TO HIS VOICE*) Be quiet will you!

MARY   It's alright son...

CHRISTINE   Is Jesus talking to you?

GEORGE   NO! There's this voice at the back of my head... Hey come here... I'll whisper what he's saying... (*CHRISTINE LEANS OVER, GEORGE WHISPERS, SHE STRAIGHTENS UP AND HITS HIM*

You've Got Me Singing The Blues

ROUND THE HEAD)

CHRISTINE	You dirty old man...
MARY	He's at it again...
COLIN-DOUGLAS	I'm warning you George...
CHRISTINE	(TO GEORGE) My body isn't for sale right? To you or anybody... (TO COLIN) Colin-Douglas, I want to go now...
COLIN-DOUGLAS	In a minute... (TO GEORGE) You watch yourself...
GEORGE	It wasn't me... it was the voice...
MARY	(TO CHRISTINE) Ignore him... I know what he's like...
COLIN-DOUGLAS	Have you paid the rent? I gave you my share...
BOBBY	So did I... it says we're four weeks behind...
STUART	It's a protest...
GEORGE	I'm sorry... I need help...
MARY	You do and all...
COLIN-DOUGLAS	Just a minute... (TO STUART) What do you mean a protest?
STUART	The rats... we shouldn't have to pay rent until the rats have been cleared out... I told them...
BOBBY	It's not rats, it's dogs...
STUART	(TAKING THE BAG FROM HIS POCKET AND EMPTIES A PILE OF CAT SHIT ONTO THE FLOOR)...What's that then? Horse manure? (THE OTHERS RECOIL)
COLIN-DOUGLAS	You didn't pay the rent because of the rats? It

took us months to get that house...

STUART You've got to stand up for your rights otherwise they'll walk all over you... We've got proof... well haven't we.

MARY That's from a cat... I know what cat shit looks like...

STUART It isn't... (SCRAPING THE BITS BACK INTO THE BAG) I know what it is and the council will have to clean out the yard...

BOBBY What happened to the money?

COLIN-DOUGLAS Have you drunk it?

STUART No... I've got it...

COLIN-DOUGLAS Show us!

STUART (TAKING AN ENVELOPE OUT OF HIS POCKET) It's in here... (COLIN–DOUGLAS SNATCHES IT FROM HIM) What are you doing?

COLIN-DOUGLAS Counting it... I knew we should have paid our own shares.

STUART Give it back...! (TRIES TO SNATCH IT BACK AND A SCUFFLE FOLLOWS... BOBBY INTERVENES, ENDS UP HOLDING THE MONEY)

BOBBY Right, I've got it... I'll count it... (BEGINS TO DO SO)

STUART It's all there...

CHRISTINE Colin-Douglas... can we go now?

COLIN-DOUGLAS In a moment...

STUART Fighting over pieces of paper... pathetic

BOBBY There's thirty quid missing...

You've Got Me Singing The Blues

GEORGE Thirty pounds... what are we going to do?

COLIN-DOUGLAS Where is it Stuart?

STUART (*TAKING A WAD FROM HIS POCKET*) Here... I was going to buy a pair of shoes...

COLIN-DOUGLAS With our rent?

STUART Why not, you're going to London... why shouldn't I have a decent pair of shoes eh?

BOBBY What happened to Oxfam? Good enough for the rest of us...

STUART That's all we bloody get, handouts... second hand stuff...

MARY Thirty pounds on a pair of shoes... you could buy a lot of food with thirty pounds...

COLIN-DOUGLAS Right give it back... come on

STUART (*MOVING AWAY FROM THEM TO ONE SIDE*) No... this is mine... I'm keeping it... it's my share of the rent...

COLIN-DOUGLAS Give it back! (*STUART TAKES OUT A CIGARETTE LIGHTER AND SETS FIRE TO THE MONEY*) What are you doing?

STUART I'll go to Oxfam and get my shoes there but this is my money... they're just pieces of paper... stuff them... stuff you...

COLIN-DOUGLAS We'll be evicted if we don't pay the rent... STOP HIM... (*HE CHASES AFTER HIM BUT STUART EVADES HIM, HOLDING UP THE FLAMING MONEY*)

GEORGE I need my injection ... Mary?

MARY It's alright George... Stuart's having a bit of a do now...

GEORGE	I like the house... it's better than the hospital...
COLIN-DOUGLAS	(TO STUART) You can't stand it when you're not the centre of attention can you eh?
STUART	You just don't understand... if we keep our noses clean, do as the doctors tell us, we might be alright... we might get an extra scrap from the table...
COLIN-DOUGLAS	It's people like you who ruin the system for everyone else... get rid of the scroungers and they could look after us properly...
STUART	Shite... there's nothing for us and there never will be... we walk the streets with nothing to do... wearing old clothes, other people's shoes... It's not going to change...
COLIN-DOUGLAS	You don't know that...
STUART	I DO!
BOBBY	Stuart man, they'll put you away again...
STUART	What difference does it make!
COLIN-DOUGLAS	(TO CHRISTINE) Come on then... (THEY TURN TO GO)
STUART	You can't go now...
COLIN-DOUGLAS	Why not?
STUART	Because, you'll need the money from the trip to pay the rent if you don't want to be evicted... hah hah... eh... that's right isn't it?
COLIN-DOUGLAS	Is that why you did it... to stop me from going to London...
STUART	Hah hah... well you can't go now... can you eh? hah hah...

You've Got Me Singing The Blues

BOBBY	I'm away... I've had enough...
GEORGE	What's going to happen Bobby?
BOBBY	I don't know George... looks like we'll be homeless again... (*EXITS*)
MARY	(*TO GEORGE*) Come on... I'll take you to see the psychiatrist... get you your injection.
GEORGE	I don't want to be homeless... (*MARY AND GEORGE EXIT*)
STUART	They'll find you somewhere... they have to...
COLIN-DOUGLAS	Right... (*TAKES CHRISTINE AWAY*)
CHRISTINE	Goodbye... Stuart pet...
STUART	You can't go!
COLIN-DOUGLAS	Watch! (*THEY EXIT*)
STUART	We've got to fight back... it's only money... Christine! I met you first... I met you first! (*THEY EXIT... HE IS LEFT ALONE*) Don't go to London... we've got to fight back... (*SONG*)

Act Two

Scene Five

GEORGE   *Now this is the coach to London and Colin and Christine are settling down. It's midnight on Monday and I play the steward in this bit.*
(COLIN AND CHRISTINE SIT DOWN SIDE BY SIDE)
Sandwiches, coffee,...sandwiches, coffee... and of course the video... sandwiches, coffee...

COLIN-DOUGLAS   Just like a plane isn't it?

CHRISTINE   There's not much room...

GEORGE   Sandwiches... coffee?

COLIN-DOUGLAS   No thanks... (*TO CHRISTINE*) I'm not paying those prices...

CHRISTINE   What time will we get there?

GEORGE   About seven in the morning...

CHRISTINE   That's a long time...

COLIN-DOUGLAS   Well, we'll have to get some sleep... won't we?

GEORGE   Do you want to watch the video?...The Evil Dead...

CHRISTINE   What's that?

GEORGE   The video!

CHRISTINE   What is it?

GEORGE   The Evil Dead... lots of blood and guts, get you off to sleep...

You've Got Me Singing The Blues

COLIN-DOUGLAS   No thank you... (*TO CHRISTINE*) Do you want some coffee... I've got a flask... or some sandwiches... I've made some... (*RUMMAGES AROUND IN HIS SUITCASE, PRODUCES SOME SANDWICHES*) Want one?

CHRISTINE   No... I think I'll go to sleep... (*LEANS AGAINST COLIN-DOUGLAS*)

COLIN-DOUGLAS   (*EATING SANDWICH*) Aye well... you sleep then... it's alright this... good to get away and tomorrow the sights of London. The Tower, Buckingham Palace, The Houses of Parliament... I am envious of people who can afford to jet away to Tenerife, I mean if you never have a holiday, life never changes does it; I certainly showed Stuart... hah hah... mind, he'll have to find that money...

CHRISTINE   I like Stuart...

COLIN-DOUGLAS   Well, I don't know why... he's uncouth...

CHRISTINE   Oh he's not refined like you Colin-Douglas...

COLIN-DOUGLAS   It's what you're brought up to be used to isn't it? I come from a good family... that's the difference...

CHRISTINE   Aren't all families good?

COLIN-DOUGLAS   No, what I mean is... well my family had standards... they didn't go out on drinking binges and blow all their money... no no, they saved and looked after their money...

CHRISTINE   And where do they live now?

COLIN-DOUGLAS   They're both dead... my father was a solicitor in Bristol... well known he was...

CHRISTINE   My family... we never had much...

COLIN-DOUGLAS   Mm... I have a sister...

CHRISTINE   I have three sisters and two brothers...

COLIN-DOUGLAS   Where do they live?

CHRISTINE   Most of them live in Sunderland...

COLIN-DOUGLAS   I've never seen any of them... do they visit you?

CHRISTINE   No, they disowned me when I was... well... when I was ill... I have been to see them but they've all got their own lives now...

COLIN-DOUGLAS   Well we've got our own life haven't we eh? Off on our holidays...

CHRISTINE   That's right (*PAUSE*) Your parents were well off... you must have some money then...?

COLIN-DOUGLAS   Well, they were comfortable... I have my share, I'm waiting for a good time to spend it...

CHRISTINE   When will that be?

COLIN-DOUGLAS   When I've found something to spend it on... when I'm back on my feet... use it to start up a business... Travel Agent perhaps, then I could spend the time going away to look at holiday resorts... imagine that, flying off to the sun, living at the best hotels and getting paid for it... why not? Unemployment's going down, I read that in the papers... when it's gone right down, people like us will be able to get a job... I've got skills you know, I used to be a fireman, mind I didn't like it much. I used to like putting the uniform on and riding to the fire with the siren going... but the flames scared me and the screaming...

CHRISTINE   Screaming?

COLIN-DOUGLAS   At the fire... people trapped, people watching... the smell of burning... I never liked that...

You've Got Me Singing The Blues

	There's lots of other things I could do... I was good at woodwork when I was at school. Mind, my father he wanted me to be a lawyer like him but... I never liked learning things out of books... work with my hands...
CHRISTINE	So you could help Stuart out then...
COLIN-DOUGLAS	I could but I'm not going to... He's only got himself to blame...
CHRISTINE	That's what they said about me...
COLIN-DOUGLAS	Who?
CHRISTINE	My family... they said I deserved to lose my bairns because of the way I went on... it's my own fault... I'm a bad person, I was punished...
COLIN-DOUGLAS	That's different to Stuart...
CHRISTINE	Your sister, what does she do?
COLIN-DOUGLAS	She's a doctor... (*CHRISTINE LOOKS SURPRISED*) yep yep... a doctor, lives in Southampton... married, two children... you know...
CHRISTINE	Could we go and see her? I like children...
COLIN-DOUGLAS	Well...
CHRISTINE	You're ashamed of me...
COLIN-DOUGLAS	No... no, it's not that... it's just well, she's busy and I haven't seen her for a while that's all...
CHRISTINE	I don't suppose she visits you...
COLIN-DOUGLAS	Oh, she does... well she did once about eight years ago but she's busy... and so am I... I go and see her now and again... when I've got nothing else on...

CHRISTINE   I'd like to see the children...

COLIN-DOUGLAS   Mm... better get some sleep eh... (*THEY SETTLE DOWN TO SLEEP... SONG*)

You've Got Me Singing The Blues

Scene Six
ENTER GEORGE FOLLOWED BY STUART AND BOBBY

GEORGE   *George is asleep, Stuart is drunk in this scene.*

STUART   *Another day has passed. Stuart has collected his giro and spent most of the evening drinking. It is now eleven o'clock on Tuesday night* (BOBBY PLAYS 'THERE'S A MAN WORKS DOWN THE CHIP-SHOP SWEARS HE'S ELVIS')

STUART   Ahh man... it's all shite... the whole thing...

BOBBY   Ssh!

STUART   What?

BOBBY   George man...

STUART   He's had his injection... you could knock the house down and he'd not wake up... (BOBBY PLAYS ON THE HARP, STUART LISTENS) Hey Bobby, that's a song about a schizophrenic (BOBBY STOPS AND LOOKS CONFUSED) There's a guy works down the chip shop swears he's Elvis; he's a liar and I'm not sure about you... Hah hah hah

BOBBY   (LAUGHING) Aye... it is like... me I prefer the blues...

STUART   Hey... Bobby, come here man... (BOBBY GOES OVER) I used to be schizophrenic but we're alright now... hah hah hah...

BOBBY   Hah hah... we're alright now... hah hah... Hey John Wayne gets off the train at central station right? He gets into a taxi and the driver says... Where do you want to go big John... and John Wayne says Westerhope...

STUART   Westerhope...hah, hah, hah... (BOTH LAUGH AT THIS JOKE) aye... this bloke visits a looney bin right and he meets this bloke in there and

	says to him 'Who are you' and the bloke says 'I am Napoleon Bonaparte...'
BOBBY	Napoleon hah hah...
STUART	Yeah... He says...'I am Napoleon Bonaparte' and the visitor says 'Napoleon? How can you be sure of that and the lunatic says 'God told me' and this voice from the next room says 'I never said any such thing...' hah hah... get it... (*BOBBY PLAYS ON HIS HARP AGAIN, STUART TAKES A DRINK FROM HIS BOTTLE*) Hey Bobby you should try this... it makes you feel better...
BOBBY	Not me man... Tea... that's my tipple
STUART	Have you never drank then?
BOBBY	Why aye... when I was in the army...
STUART	Oh aye... Northern Ireland wasn't it?
BOBBY	Aye, ten years ago... before I went loopy and they came and took me away... held me down and whoop... (*MIMICS SOMEONE INJECTING HIM IN HIS ARM*)
STUART	Ireland... we should get our troops out of there...
BOBBY	Smuggling... that's what the IRA were interested in... right bloody racket...
STUART	Anyone killed?
BOBBY	Oh aye... we lost three men and a cow...
STUART	A cow...?
BOBBY	We were sitting in this field for hours on end... waiting for the IRA to attack... hour after hour... me with this bloody great machine gun... I got bored...

You've Got Me Singing The Blues

STUART   What happened?

BOBBY   I took aim...

STUART   Yeh yeh? And?

BOBBY   I shot this cow...

STUART   You did... hah hah... Killed it?

BOBBY   Oh aye... hah hah... made a bloody hell of a racket though... jumping around (*MIMICS THE NOISE AND MOVEMENTS OF THE DOOMED ANIMAL, STUART LAUGHS*)...hah hah.

STUART   Did you get into trouble?

BOBBY   Aye... they took away me stripes... I was a corporal... you know... (*PLAYS ON HIS HARP*)

STUART   And the men you lost... what happened?

BOBBY   Blown up... all three... standing round this car and up it went... insides blown to bits...

STUART   We're all crazy now eh Bobby... Repent for the end is nigh... (*SINGS*) 'They're coming to take me away hah hah to the funny farm...' (*HE CAVORTS AROUND AND THEN STOPS AND LOOKS AT BOBBY*)
You never let things get to you, do you...?

BOBBY   Keep me head down... avoid getting worked up... otherwise we get ill...

STUART   Ill... schizo eh? What does it mean to be schizo?

BOBBY   (*TAPPING HIS HEAD*) Something wrong in here...

STUART   That's what they tell us but who's to say the one's telling us haven't got something wrong in here... (*TAPS HIS HEAD*)

BOBBY	They don't hear voices and behave badly...
STUART	What's worse eh Bobby? Pressing the button that fires a nuclear missile or directing the traffic in Northumberland Street in your underpants... eh... hah hah, I did that once... (STUART DROPS HIS TROUSERS AND MIMES DIRECTING TRAFFIC WHILE BOBBY LAUGHS)
BOBBY	Did you... hah hah... I knew a bloke did something like that... topped himself in the end like...
STUART	Don't blame him... (SINGS LINE FROM KIRSTY MCCOLL SONG AGAIN AND TAKES A DRINK)...Did you know you're eight times more likely to be diagnosed schizophrenic if you're poor than if you're rich.
BOBBY	Does that mean if we get rich, we get better... hah hah... Except you've got to eat the money, that's the medication... hah hah... hey...
STUART	No man, the medication is having money and being able to spend it... the drugs they give us, they're just to control us... keep us down...
BOBBY	No Stuart man, we need the medication...
STUART	Do we?
BOBBY	Well look at George... he does... And you go funny if you don't have yours...
STUART	I'm going to stop taking my medication... stick with this instead... (BRANDISHING THE BOTTLE)
BOBBY	Women... I'd like to know a woman... hah hah eh Stuart?
STUART	Ever been to bed with a man Bobby?

BOBBY	Me no... hah hah... not me...
STUART	What's wrong with it...?
BOBBY	Nothing...
STUART	This society can't stand anyone who's different... like us eh?
BOBBY	You like Christine though...
STUART	I'll not see her again...
BOBBY	Don't be daft man... You'll see her tomorrow...
STUART	How do you know?
BOBBY	I saw Colin's ticket... they went down on the coach last night and they'll be coming back on the coach tonight...
STUART	They're just there for the day?
BOBBY	That's right...
STUART	Hah hah hah... he was going to get a job and a flat and... stupid bugger... hah hah... I wish I'd known... why didn't you say anything?
BOBBY	He was enjoying himself...
STUART	Aye with Christine... does she know it's only for a day?
BOBBY	Don't know...
STUART	Stupid bugger... (BEGINS TO SING OVER AND OVER AGAIN, 'COLIN'S A STUPID BUGGER' GETTING LOUDER AND LOUDER WHEN MARY ENTERS)
MARY	Hello you lot... drinking again... how's George? (GOING OVER TO LOOK AT HIM) Are you alright pet?

BOBBY	You didn't like him the other day...
MARY	When?
BOBBY	When he kissed you eh hah hah...
MARY	You twisty headed bugger... it's not his fault... it's his voices...
STUART	Oh aye...'course... (OFFERING BOTTLE TO MARY) Want some?
MARY	No... where did you get the money for drink...
STUART	What's green and you drink it eh? Your giro... Tuesday's giro day... (DRINKING)
MARY	You should have saved your money, George is really upset...
STUART	What's it got to do with you... you don't live here...?
BOBBY	Aye, what about them cats of yours? They'll be starving...
MARY	I've been home and looked after them... don't you worry... but you Stuart, you should have saved your money...
STUART	You sound like bloody Colin... another Thatcher lover...
MARY	Don't you go attacking my friend Margaret Thatcher...
STUART	She doesn't care about people like us...
MARY	You men... you make me sick...
STUART	There's people going hungry, homeless... there's nothing done about it...
MARY	Who's going hungry? You're not... you're

	fine you are with your bottle of brown... You don't see any kids today without shoes do you eh? What you see is men in pubs getting drunk with the family allowance book in their pockets...
STUART	Why don't you go back to your cats then...
MARY	(*SOBBING*) You don't like me anymore do you eh? You're not my friends... (*CRYING, BOBBY AND STUART LAUGH AT HER*)
GEORGE	(*WAKING UP*) What's going on?
BOBBY	Alright George?
GEORGE	That bloody injection, she gave me a new drug again... I can hardly think... (*MARY IS STILL UPSET*) Hello Mary...
STUART	She's upset... she should go to her own house...
MARY	I've got as much right to be here as you... I'm schizophrenic too you know!
GEORGE	At least she's got a house to go to... we're out by Monday...
STUART	The social worker will sort it out...
MARY	She'll have you put away this time...
STUART	So what?
GEORGE	I don't want to be put away...
MARY	I wouldn't mind... they do everything for you... cook, clean... all you have to do is sit there and watch the tele... I'd like that...
GEORGE	It's these voices... I've got this little man in the middle of my forehead and he's nice... he speaks in this high pitched voice you know and he tells me things like right now he's

	telling what the weather's like in Sunderland...
STUART	Sunderland hah ha... it'll be raining there eh... hah hah...
GEORGE	Then I've got this nasty voice in the back of my head... eh shut up!
MARY	What's he saying?
GEORGE	He just doesn't stop... (*PAUSE*) Stuart can't you get that money back?
STUART	How?
GEORGE	He says you'll be punished if we're evicted...
STUART	Tell him I'll punish him then... eh Bobby... hah hah...
BOBBY	Leave him alone Stuart... he's having a bad time...
STUART	We all are... you don't care about him... not really, you only care about yourself... well we all do don't we?
MARY	Speak for yourself...
STUART	No one wants to look after us... why don't we have people who care for us, family, friends?
BOBBY	They've got their own lives to live...
GEORGE	I'm going home... (*STANDS*)
MARY	Sit down George, this is your home... (*STUART IGNORES THIS EXCHANGE, GEORGE REMAINS STANDING. HE WATCHES FOR A MOMENT, THEN EXITS*)
STUART	We don't listen... We're like a group of people in a waiting room at a bus station, we

	don't know each other... we're waiting for the ticket that's going to take us away except it never comes...
BOBBY	Waiting aye... waiting to rush...
STUART	What?
BOBBY	Waiting to rush... that's what we used to call it in the army when we were on standby... you'd be kitted up and then wait hours... maybe days and suddenly, anytime of the day or night the call would come and you'd run carrying equipment, bumping into each other with the NCO's shouting at you to get into a truck or a helicopter and rush to a place. And nine times out of ten you'd be set down in the middle of nowhere in the dark and it would be quiet and you'd be waiting again...
GEORGE	What for?
BOBBY	Anything... the next rush... ninety percent of army life is boredom...
STUART	And a hundred percent of a schizophrenic's is!
BOBBY	You've got to play the grey man...

GEORGE ENTERS IN HIS UNDERPANTS. HE CLIMBS ON A CHAIR AND BEGINS CHANTING LIKE A RED INDIAN

MARY	George!... What are you doing
STUART	(*DANCING AROUND IN SYMPATHY*) Go on George man...
BOBBY	Stuart... leave him alone...
STUART	He's getting rid of the evil spirits... praying to the medicine man...
MARY	(*PUSHING STUART AWAY*) Stop it!

Steve Chambers

STUART   Don't you push me... (*BOBBY RESTRAINS HIM AS HE IS ABOUT TO RETURN*)

BOBBY   Sit down... he's ill...

MARY   George, what are you doing?

GEORGE   Chanting...

STUART   See, I told you...

MARY   He wouldn't be like this if you hadn't worried him about the house...

STUART   Get stuffed...

GEORGE   (*JUMPING DOWN*) I need some exercise... (*STARTS DOING PRESS-UPS ENERGETICALLY*)

BOBBY   George... do you want to go to the hospital?

STUART   That's right... lock him up...

MARY   It's you should be locked up...

GEORGE   (*EXHAUSTED*) Mary... I'm not well... help me...

MARY   It's alright son...

GEORGE   I need the doctor... I need the doctor!

BOBBY   (*WITH MARY HELPING HIM UP*) Aye... don't worry... (*TO MARY*) Get his clothes on... I'll go and phone... (*MARY SITS GEORGE DOWN AND BEGINS TO DRESS HIM. HE IS BY THIS STAGE HELPLESS AND PLIANT AND HE WHIMPERS A LITTLE... BOBBY GOES TO GO AND THEN RETURNS*) Anyone got a ten pence piece?

STUART   Hah hah hah (*SONG. DURING THIS NUMBER, WE SEE GEORGE ENTERING HOSPITAL HELPED BY MARY AND BOBBY. HE IS LEFT THERE.*)

You've Got Me Singing The Blues

Scene Seven

MARY Now where are those magazines... (*LOOKS ROUND FOR THEM*) Silly old bugger said they were in this room...
(*LOOKS AT AUDIENCE*) It's Wednesday morning and Mary's in the house. She and Bobby took George to the hospital last night... Enter Stuart with a hangover (*STUART ENTERS WITH HANGOVER*) He watches Mary but she doesn't see him straight away.(*SHE TIDIES*) Tidy up a bit and then it'll be fine... plenty of chat... that's what I need...

STUART You still here? (*SITTING DOWN. MARY IGNORES HIM AND CONTINUES SEARCHING FOR THE MAGAZINES.*) What are you looking for? (*SHE CONTINUES TO IGNORE HIM*) I heard you talking to yourself before you know... you want to be careful... first sign of madness... mind you've got a few others like... (*ENTER COLIN-DOUGLAS AND CHRISTINE*)

COLIN-DOUGLAS Hello everyone... we've had a great time haven't we Christine...

CHRISTINE Lovely... hello Stuart (*GOES OVER TO HIM AND KISSES HIM. BOBBY ENTERS, READY TO GO OUT: CHRISTINE GOES OVER TO HIM AND KISSES HIM*) Hello Bobby...

BOBBY You're back then...

COLIN-DOUGLAS Aye but it does you good to get away... hey guess what, we went round Harrods and we saw a dress for £675.00. Imagine that six hundred and seventy-five pounds for one dress...

STUART Get a job then did you?

MARY Ignore him... (*SHE CONTINUES LOOKING FOR SOME MAGAZINES*)

STUART He said he was going to get a job and a flat

	and all sorts... mind I suppose it's difficult if you only go for the day...
COLIN-DOUGLAS	We decided to come back, well we'd seen everything, hadn't we Christine? We'll go for longer next time...
STUART	Huh!
COLIN-DOUGLAS	Well, what did you do yesterday eh?
MARY	Drink... can't you tell, he's got a bad head haven't you son...
COLIN-DOUGLAS	Typical...
STUART	Don't start on me with your tory morality...
CHRISTINE	We prayed in some lovely churches... Colin-Douglas took me all over...
COLIN-DOUGLAS	And everywhere we went, Christine wanted to pray... on the underground... she had them all singing in this compartment...
BOBBY	Get in... hah hah... what was that...'Abide with Me'...hah hah...
COLIN-DOUGLAS	Not just on the underground... in the Wimpy Bar and the pubs... mind the prices of things... seventy-five pence for a bloody ice-cream... over a pound for a pint of beer...
BOBBY	You had a good time then?
COLIN-DOUGLAS	Oh aye... mind I've changed my mind about living there... you'd have to earn a fortune to afford things... I think you've got to get started somewhere cheaper like Newcastle and then move when you're on your feet you know... (*PAUSE*) Where's George?
BOBBY	In the hospital...

MARY	Took bad last night... I'm taking him some things... (FINDS THE MAGAZINES, STARTS TO LOOK AT THEM) The dirty old bugger... (LOOKS UP) Filth!
STUART	Hah hah... George's dirty books, therapy...
MARY	You're all the same... I'm not taking them...
STUART	That's it... deprive him of his last remaining pleasure...
BOBBY	George'll manage, he's got a lot of imagination that lad... hah hah...
COLIN-DOUGLAS	You haven't sorted out the rent then?
STUART	Don't come back here and start getting at me... right?
BOBBY	I'm off out... do a bit of busking...
COLIN-DOUGLAS	You can't go... this is an important discussion, it concerns the house...
BOBBY	You haven't got the rent, I haven't... Stuart hasn't... what're we going to do?
CHRISTINE	Colin-Douglas is going to help Stuart aren't you?
COLIN-DOUGLAS	Well, I said I might...
STUART	That'll be the day...
CHRISTINE	The day of reckoning when we shall all be made to pay for our sins...
STUART	Look it'll be alright... there'll be a bit of hassle, it'll blow over... what can they do?
MARY	They'll put you in the hospital son...
STUART	Give it a rest...

CHRISTINE   (*TO COLIN-DOUGLAS*) You said you would help him... you've got money...

COLIN-DOUGLAS   Yes... but I don't think it's a good idea...

CHRISTINE   If you love me, you'll help him...

BOBBY   It's alright Christine love... don't worry about us...

CHRISTINE   He promised to help me find Loraine Marie...

COLIN-DOUGLAS   It's difficult in one day... we did look, London's a big place...

CHRISTINE   You don't care...

COLIN-DOUGLAS   We'll look next time...

CHRISTINE   When... when?

COLIN-DOUGLAS   Stop shouting at me will you?

CHRISTINE   HELP STUART!

COLIN-DOUGLAS   I CAN'T! (*PAUSE*) I can't... I haven't got any money... I just said that. We were having a nice time...

STUART   And you wanted to impress her...

CHRISTINE   You lied to me, that's evil...

COLIN-DOUGLAS   We had a nice time... I bought you a present... and I paid for everything...

CHRISTINE   That's all you're bloody interested in... isn't it? (*TAKING THE PRESENT FROM HER BAG. IT IS A MODEL OF THE TOWER OF LONDON*) Here have it back... (*THROWS IT AT HIM, EXITS*)

COLIN-DOUGLAS   Christine... (*GOING AFTER HIM*)...Christine... (*HE RETURNS*) She's gone... (*TO STUART*) It's all your fault...

You've Got Me Singing The Blues

STUART How do you work that out, anyway she doesn't mean it...

COLIN-DOUGLAS Do you want a fight then eh?

STUART Calm down will you...

BOBBY She'll be upset... it was her kid's birthday you know...

COLIN-DOUGLAS What are you going to do about the rent then?

STUART Talk to the social worker... try and explain...

COLIN-DOUGLAS That'll take some doing...

STUART I could do with a drink...

MARY Already?

STUART It's about time you went to see George isn't it? Took him those magazines... Well go on... (*MARY DOESN'T MOVE*)

COLIN-DOUGLAS (*TO STUART*) You spoil everything don't you...

STUART Leave me alone will you... (*TO MARY*) What are you waiting for?

MARY Can I stay... while George is in hospital... I'll tidy up...

STUART What here? (*MARY NODS*)

BOBBY You can stay for me Mary...

STUART Not if she's going to report me to the social worker she can't...

COLIN-DOUGLAS There won't be anywhere to stay if we're evicted...

MARY I'd just like someone to talk to now and again... I get lonely you know...

COLIN-DOUGLAS   But we haven't got the rent... oh I know Stuart says he'll talk to the social worker but she might decide enough's enough... after all, we've had some problems before...

STUART   I've told you, I'll sort it out...

COLIN-DOUGLAS   How? Tell me that...

STUART   Shut up and stop getting at me...

COLIN-DOUGLAS   It's your own fault...

MARY   I've got some money... (*RUMMAGING IN BAG*)

BOBBY   What?

MARY   It's here somewhere...

STUART   How much?

MARY   My sister gave me some at Christmas to buy a carpet...

BOBBY   You're always going on about having no money...

MARY   It's only fifty pounds... (*FINDS THE MONEY*) it seemed too much to spend you know... when you're used to having nothing... anyway, my memory's bad... I forget things...

STUART   Bugger me... Let's have it then and I'll go down the council offices...

COLIN-DOUGLAS   You're not having it... not after last time... I'll go and I'll tell them there aren't any rats...

STUART   There are!

BOBBY   Leave it Stuart...

COLIN-DOUGLAS   Have you got the rest Bobby?

BOBBY	Aye, I'll come with you Colin, then I'll do a bit of busking... (*COLIN-DOUGLAS AND BOBBY EXIT*)
STUART	(*AFTER THEM*) You'll regret it when we all come down with rat born illnesses...
MARY	I'll go and see George... (*EXITS LEAVING MAGAZINES BEHIND*)
STUART	Fancy a drink on the way you two? (*THEY LOOK AT HIM AND EXIT. STUART SHOUTS AFTER THEM*) All's well that ends well eh...? (*EXITS AFTER THEM. MARY REAPPEARS AND COMES BACK. SHE PICKS UP THE MAGAZINES AND EXAMINES THEM*)
MARY	Dirty old bugger... suppose I'd better take them... (*SHOVES THEM INTO HER BAG AND EXITS*)

Scene Eight

GEORGE *George isn't asleep this time, he's drugged... he'll be in the hospital for a few weeks now... Mary comes to visit him... (ENTER MARY)*

MARY (*FURTIVELY GETTING MAGAZINES FROM A CARRIER BAG*) Here you are you old bugger... (*KISSES HIM*)...You'd better not let them see these... (*PUTS THEM UNDER HIS BLANKET*) I'll put them under there... now... how are you? (*SITS NEXT TO HIM*)

GEORGE Hello... Mary?

MARY That's it... I'm here... now you're not to worry about the house, that's all been sorted out... I'm going to stay there. I'll keep an eye on things don't you worry... and I'll have someone to chat to... aye I'll keep them all in order... and I'll come and see you... when you're feeling better... *Mary stayed there for quite a while talking to him, then walked him back to his ward.* (*HELPS GEORGE OFF*)

BOBBY (*BOBBY MOVES TO THE FRONT OF THE STAGE, REMOVES HIS HAVERSACK, CAP AND MAC, TAKES OUT HIS FLASK AND POURS HIMSELF A CUP OF TEA, THEN HE ROLLS A CIGARETTE... ALL THIS AS HE IS SPEAKING*)
This is my place... under the Tyne Bridge... You can sit on your own and watch the world go by... down here... there's the sky, the birds and down there two dogs worrying a dead pigeon... nobody takes any notice... me, I play the grey man.
If anyone ever says to me 'Go to hell', I say I don't need to... I've been there... oh aye. The bad times like George is having well, you wouldn't wish that on anyone... your mind it goes haywire... you see and hear things that aren't there and yet for you they are there, they're real, it's just nobody else knows what you're on about and that's when you get

scared, really bloody scared, because you're not in charge of your own mind... You start to question everything... is that bridge really there or the pavement?
We've all had them but we don't like talking about them... no, that's the last thing you want to do... but it's there haunting you and you wonder when it's going to happen again...
Stay calm... that's the trick, play the grey man... that's what we used to call it in the army when we were waiting hour after hour in some lonely place in the dark for something, pretending you don't exist, slowed down, like in a trance. Aye that was the trick; you'd go crackers otherwise. That's what you've got to do if you're schizophrenic, play the grey man otherwise you end up like George.
Trouble is, unlike the army, you've got to do it all the time... (*TAKES OUT HARMONICA AND BEGINS TO PLAY. THIS BECOMES THE LAST SONG OF THE SHOW*)